Ralph Waldo Trine

The greatest thing ever known

Ralph Waldo Trine

The greatest thing ever known

ISBN/EAN: 9783337221768

Printed in Europe, USA, Canada, Australia, Japan

Cover: Foto ©Andreas Hilbeck / pixelio.de

More available books at **www.hansebooks.com**

THE GREATEST THING
EVER KNOWN

THE GREATEST THING EVER KNOWN

By

RALPH WALDO TRINE

The moment we fully and vitally realize WHO AND WHAT WE ARE, *we then begin to build our own world even as God builds His*

NEW YORK

THOMAS Y. CROWELL & CO.

PUBLISHERS

CONTENTS

THE GREATEST THING EVER KNOWN

I

THE greatest thing ever known—What is it? Full surely the answer must be one that is absolutely universal, both in its nature and in the possibilities of its application. It must be one that can be accepted wholly and unreservedly, not only by a single individual, but even by bodies of individuals, be they the originators of any particular school of Ethics, the followers of any particular system of Philosophy, or even the adherents of any great system of Religion. It must be one so true in itself that it can be accepted by all men alike the world over.

And again, it must be an answer that is true for no particular period of time, but equally true for all time—an answer that was true not only for yesterday, that is true for to-day, that may be true for to-morrow,

A

but one equally true for yesterday, to-day, and forever. In laying our foundation, therefore, it must be laid upon something as true and as certain as Life itself, and as eternal as Everlasting Life.

What is as true and as certain as Life itself? Life, only Life. And what do we mean by this answer? Let us give it for a moment our most careful consideration, for upon what we find here depends and rests all that is to follow. Let us start, then, with that in regard to which all can agree; something taken not from mere tradition, from mere hearsay, but something that comes to us from no source other than our own interior consciousness, our own reason and insight. In other words, let us make our approach, not from the theological stand-point, but from that which is far more certain and satisfactory—the philosophical.

Then, and then only, will we allow pure reason to be our guide, and then by having as the earnest desire of both mind and heart, truth, truth for its own sake, and then for the sake of its influence upon every-day life, we will thus allow pure reason to be illumined by the Light that lighteth every man that cometh into the world. In the degree that we open ourselves to and are true to this are we on sure and safe ground, for thus are we going directly to the source and the only source of all *true* revelation. In the degree, on the other hand, that we close ourselves or become untrue to this are we on uncertain and dangerous ground, and liable to find ourselves hopelessly floundering in the quagmire of theological traditions and speculations and doubts, of which the world has already seen so much. Pure reason, therefore, shall be our guide—pure reason illumined by the Inner Light.

Again, then, What is Life? Being is Life. Life is Being. Being, therefore, is our starting-point, and indeed our very foundation itself.

Each can form his own idea of Being, so that in reality it needs no defining. By it we mean that self-existent principle of Life and all that attends it, without beginning and without end, the Power that animates all and so that is the Life of all. In short, we can scarcely define Being, if indeed it can be defined, without using the word Life, and indeed without identifying the two.

Being and Life, then, are one and the same.

It is Being that projects itself into ex-istence. Being, acting through its own intelligence, prompted by love, projected by will, goes out and *takes* form. We cannot say that it enters into form, for until it projects itself into existence *there is no form*, but form comes by virtue of Being, the self-existent Principle of Life and Power manifesting itself in existence. So in a sense Life, which is one with Being, is the soul, and form, of whatever nature the body.

Only as Being projects itself into existence are we able to know it. We can know the fact that Being *is*, but only as it manifests itself in form are we able to know *it itself*.

Being is *one*, not many. As Being is the source of all Life, there is, then, only one Life, and this Being is the Life of all. "The one Divine Being; and this alone is the true Reality in all Existence, and so remains in all Eternity." And there is nothing *real* that is, or, indeed, that can be, outside of it. True, then, are the words of one of the most highly illumined philosophers of modern

times—"Thus we have these two elements:
Being, as it is essentially and in itself; and
Form, which is assumed by the former in
consequence of Existence. But how have
we expressed ourselves? What is it that
assumes a form? Answer: Being, as it
exists in itself, without any change whatever in its inward, Essential Nature. But
what, then, is there in Existence? Answer:
Nothing else than the One Eternal and
Unchangeable Being, besides which there
can be nothing."

This Being which is Infinite is in truth,
then, the Infinite Being, and this Infinite
Being is what we mean by God—each using
the term that appeals most to himself.
Literally, the I Am, as is signified by the
name Jehovah, which is derived in the
Hebrew from the word To Be. God, then,
is the Infinite Being, the Infinite Spirit of
Life which fills all in existence with himself
alone, so that all is He, since He is All. If
God is all, then all *must* be He, and from
this fact there is no escape, and no other
conclusion can be arrived at which does not
do violence to all rational thought. There
are those—and to such these pages are not

addressed, for so limited are they in comprehension, or so closed to truth and hence
so engrossed in bigotry, that they either can
or will see nothing that may be opposed to
their present ideas—there are those who say
that God is all, and immediately begin to fill
up the universe with that which God is not.

Again, there are those open to and eagerly
seeking for the highest truth who say: But
evil is not God, and how then can God be
all, for surely there is such a thing as evil.
Certainly evil is not God, nor has God anything to do with evil. Evil is simply the
result of the temporary perversion of the
good, and as such must either cease or in
time die at its own hands. As such, then,
it has no *essential* reality, for that which has
essential reality has neither beginning nor
end.

Man is the only one who has to do with
evil, he alone is its author; man, who in his
thought separates himself from Divine Being,
in whom alone true happiness and blessedness can be found. Regarding the mere
bodily existence as his real life, he tries to
find pleasure and happiness entirely through
these channels, and many times by violating

the higher laws of his being, and thus what we term evil enters in. But though man has perfect freedom in all his thoughts and acts, God will suffer no such violation. And so, from the pain and suffering that result from the violation of the higher laws of his being, he is pushed on in his thought and through this in his life to the Reality of his being, and finds that only in conscious union with God true pleasure and blessedness lie, as God surely intends. True, then, evil is not God, nor has God anything to do with evil; for man alone has to do with it, so long, and only so long, as he lives his life out of a conscious union with the life of God.

Infinite Being, God, then, is the one and the only Life. You and I in our true selves are Life. It cannot be truly said that we *have* life, for we *are* Life; Life that manifests itself in the form in existence that we denominate by the term body. And as the Infinite Being, the Infinite Life, God, is the I Am, the life of all in existence, then we indeed are parts of the Infinite Being, the Infinite Life, the I Am, of the very God himself. And thus it is that your life and

mine is one with the life of God. By this
we do not mean the mere body, but the
Real Self that takes to itself the form—
body. It is utterly impossible that there
be any real life that is not one with the
life of God. And in this sense it is true
that the life of man and the life of God
are essentially and necessarily one and the
same. In essence they are one and the
same ; they differ not in quality, for this it
is impossible rationally even to conceive of.
There is a difference—it is a difference
simply in *degree*, not in essence or kind.
It is only by reason of our own thought
that our life is separate from the life of
God, only by reason of our own thought
that we live in this separation, if indeed
we can use the term *live* where the *full*
life is not consciously realised and enjoyed.
Truly, then, "In Him we live and move
and have our being."

We never could have been, and never can
be, other than Divine Being. And I fully
agree with the thought expressed in a recent
letter from Prof. Max Müller in which
he says : " I cannot accept Athanasius
when he says that we can become gods ;

man cannot say, become God, because he is God; what else could he be, if God is the only true and real being?"

How is it, then, I hear it asked, that man has the limitations that he has, that he is subject to fears and forebodings, that he is liable to sin and error, that he is the victim of disease and suffering? There is but one reason. He is not living, except in rare cases here and there, in the *conscious realisation* of his own true Being, and hence of his own true Self. We must *in thought* be conscious of who and what we are before the qualities and powers of our real being, and hence our real selves, actualise or even manifest themselves. Says one of the most highly illumined seers of modern times: "The True Life and its Blessedness consists in a union with the Unchangeable and Eternal; but the Eternal can be apprehended *only by Thought*, and is in no other way approachable by us."

Thought is the atmosphere, the element, in a sense the very substance, of the phase of Divine Being that we call human life. How much it is likewise that of other forms of Divine Being in existence, as we see it in the various manifestations of life around us, we cannot be so fully certain of. But certain it is that through thought, and through thought alone, we are able to conceive of Divine Being as the Infinite Spirit and Essence of Life, and then to see clearly that it is the Life of our Life, and then to live in the realisation of our oneness with it, and in this way allow the Divine Word to become incarnate in us by being thus fully and completely manifest in us, precisely as it became manifest and hence incarnate in the Christ Jesus, as we shall hereafter find.

When Divine Being manifests itself in physical human form, its inward essential nature or reality changes not, for this from its very nature it is impossible for it in any way to do. It does, however, have to manifest itself through the agency of physical senses, and precisely for this reason is it that for a time our real inward Essential Nature and Life is concealed from us, but this again only by reason of our limited comprehension.

When we are born into the world of Nature we see and cognise through and by means of the physical senses, and the natural physical world becomes to us for a time the *real* world. By-and-by, however, through these very senses we are able to conceive of the One and Eternal Source of Life as our real and therefore our only life, and then through them to hold ourselves in this living realisation.   Hence, first that which is natural and *then* that which is spiritual is necessarily as well as literally and philosophically true.   Happy, however, is the man who dwells not long as the purely natural man, but is early transformed into the spiritual, and so in whom the Divine Word early becomes incarnate.

Blessed state indeed, says the thoughtful and earnest seeker for the best things in life, and more to be prized than all else besides; but if this state is really possible of realisation, what can be said regarding the method of entering into it?   There is only one thing in all the wide universe that will enable you, as well as all the world, to do it effectually.   "Be ye therefore transformed by the renewing of your minds." This is the force, the transforming power, so far as the form of life we denominate by the term human is concerned, this and this alone.

True, then, and most welcome is the great fact of facts, of which the world is beginning to become so conscious to-day, that "The mind is everything; what you think, you become." Mortal mind? says one. Yes and no. Strictly speaking, there is no such thing as mortal mind—there is only Divine Mind. When in our own thought, and by reason of our limited comprehension, we shut ourselves off and look upon ourselves as individual physical beings, we give birth to a temporary mode of thought that might well be termed mortal mind, or, rather, the product of mortal mind. But it is at first natural, and it is only by using this "mortal mind" that it is able to be transformed, and hence re-newed into the Divine Mind. So by wisely using that which we have, the natural, we are transformed from that which is most apparent, and consequently that which we think we are, the mortal, the physical, into that which from all eternity we in reality are, and never except in our own minds can get away from, — the Spiritual, the Divine.

It is through this instrumentality that the Divine Life within us, the Divine Life with all its ever-ready-to-break-forth glories and powers, is enabled to be changed from a mere passive and hence potential actuality, and to burst forth into the full splendours of conscious, active life. Surely, then, thought rightly directed and rightly used has within it the true regenerating and hence redeeming power; through it and it alone are we able to make for ourselves a new heaven and a new earth, or, rather, by thus finding the kingdom of God, and through it entering into the conscious realisation of the heavenly state, are we able to make for ourselves a new earth by actualising the kingdom of Heaven in our lives while living on the earth, which, when once truly realised, can never be lost.

The majority of people are not awake; it is only here and there that we find one even partially awake. Practically all of us, as a result, are living lives that are unworthy almost the name of lives, compared with those we might be living, and that lie within

our easy grasp.   While it is true that each
life is in and of Divine Being, hence always
one with it, in order that this great fact may
bear fruit in individual lives, each one must,
as we have already said, be conscious of it,
he must know it in thought, and then live
continually in this consciousness.

An eagle has been chained for many
months to the perch just outside his cage;
so long has he been conscious of the fact
that he is bound by the little silver chain
which holds him, that he has given up all
efforts to escape, almost forgetting, perhaps,
that the power of flight is longer his.   One
day a link of the little chain opens, but,
living so long in the consciousness that he
is held in captivity, he makes no effort to
escape.   The freedom of the heavens is now
his, were he only conscious of his power.
But day after day he sits sullenly longing for
freedom, but remaining a captive still.   One
morning, however, he ventures a little farther
out on his perch than usual, when suddenly
a strange consciousness is his—he sets his
wings, and the captivity which has held him
for months will perchance know him no
more forever.

And so it is with man. On account of the false gods that tradition and prevailing theology have brought him he knows not himself, and not knowing himself he knows neither his powers nor his possibilities. The human soul is held captive. An opaque physical structure is about all that he can be said truly to give evidence of. The day comes, however, when in his thought he moves out a little farther than is usual, then a little farther and a little farther. The Inner Light is now moving within, he catches at first a little glimpse of his real Essential Being, then a little more and a little more, and by-and-by the fact of his essential oneness with the Infinite Life and Power bursts in upon, illumines, and takes possession of his soul. In bewilderment, and almost afraid to utter it at first, he cries aloud, "O God, I am one with Thee!" Enraptured by this new consciousness, he holds to the thought of this oneness, and living continually in this thought his life forever after flows steadily on in one constant realisation of his oneness with Divine Being. And so "the first man, [which] is of the earth earthy," is changed into "the second man,

[which] is the Lord from Heaven," and thereafter the Christ sits enthroned.

Compared with the new life that he is now
continually living, the old life of ignorance
with its consequent limitations, which can
now know him no more forever, deserved
only the name of death, for, in a sense, he
was indeed dead unto life, and only he who
lives in the conscious realisation of his oneness with the One and Only Life can be said
truly to be born into Life. He is born into
the world and lives in the world, but into
consciously real and eternal *Life* he has not
yet entered. He is born the Adam man,
but within him the Christ man has not
awakened, or, rather, he has not yet awakened to the Christ within, and so the Christ
man is not yet born, and sitting therefore in
darkness he knows not yet the glorious
realities of life.

"I am thine own Spirit" are the words
that the Infinite Father by means of the
Inner Voice is continually speaking to every
human soul. He who *will* hear *can* hear,
and through it step out into fulness of life.

We hear much in the prevailing crude and

irrational theology in regard to the "fall of man"; but it is only as man has departed from the Inner Light, and gone after false man-made gods, that anything that might rationally be termed a "fall" has come about. Separating our lives in thought from their oneness with Divine Life is what constitutes, and what alone will ever constitute, the fall of man. But the teaching that has come to us through past generations, which has as its dominant keynote, poor worm and miserable sinner, death and the grave, is as false as it is pernicious and therefore damnable in its influences. These old thoughts and words have had the influence of taking heaven out of earth and populating the earth with doubt, and error, and sin, and crime. New and true thoughts and words will make literally a new heaven and a new earth.

Man is essentially Divine, actually part of the Infinite God, and so, essentially good. When he severs his connection in consciousness with the Divine, then and then only do doubt, and error, and sin, and crime, with their consequent pain, suffering, disease, and despair, enter into his life. Only a pure and radical infidel—by this we mean one who is

B

in reality such, for there are many who are
called infidels, even by many avowed re-
ligionists, who live a far truer religion than
they themselves live—can rationally hold to
the doctrine of original sin, with its consequent poor worm and miserable sinner.   The
religious teacher who professes to believe in
God as the One Divine and Supreme Being,
and at the same time holds to this irrational
doctrine, is many times more a disciple of
the Devil, whom he recognises and whose
power he evidently respects, than he is of
the Infinite God in whom he *professes* to
believe.   He and he alone it is who finds a
place for what he and his theology term the
Devil.   The one who truly believes in God
as the only true and real being and the
source of all life and power can indeed find
no place for the Devil.   He sees and recognises the evil that comes from lives that lose
for a time their conscious connection with
the Supreme Source of their being, but he
can find no place for any other *essential and
abiding* Reality.

And as this separation from God is made
entirely through the instrumentality of the
mind, he sees that making one's conscious

connection again with God—the true and only true redemption—must also be through the instrumentality of the mind. Believing in the God in whom he believes, ay, *knowing the God whom he knows*, he sees no place for an atonement in the sense of appeasing the wrath of an angry God. Knowing the God whom he knows, he shares not in those barbaric notions. He does see, however, that redemption can and must come through living in the conscious at-one-ment with the Father's life. He recognises it as the natural method that the Adam man be first born, with freedom of thought and consequently freedom of action, and that from him the Christ man then comes forth into consciousness. He recognises that it is God's, and consequently nature's and evolution's method, that "the first man is of the earth earthy, the second man is the Lord from heaven." He recognises the fact that kittens are born blind, not because their parents or even their grandparents sinned, but because it is simply *natural* for them to be born blind, and that in process of time their eyes will open. He also recognises that, on account of our limited comprehension, the "natural" appears first and then the "spiritual," but in reality the spiritual is from the very first incarnated within, and only because it is, can it in process of time, either sooner or later, assume the ascendency by changing from potential into active life.

Once in a while there comes into the world one who from the very first recognises no separation of his life from the Father's life, and who dwells continually in this living realisation; and by bringing anew to the world this great fact, and showing forth the works that will always and inevitably follow this realisation, he becomes in a sense a world's saviour, as did Jesus, who, through the completeness of his realisation of the Father's life incarnate in him, became the Christ Jesus. He in this way pointed out to the world how all men can enter into the realisation of the Christ-life and thus be saved from all impulse to sin. And so instead of coming to appease the vengeance of an angry God—difficult for one who has any adequate conception of God even to conceive of—he brought to the world, by exemplifying in his own life as well as by teaching to all who will hear his *real message*, the method whereby all of us can enter into the full and complete realisation of our oneness with the life of the tender and loving Infinite Father.

Redeemed from the bondage of the senses through which alone sin comes, and born into the heavenly state, into life eternal, is every one who comes into the same relations with the Father, and hence into the same realisation of his oneness with the Father's life, that Jesus came into. It is difficult, however, to see how any one will be redeemed from the bondage of sin and enter into the heavenly state simply by believing that Jesus entered into it while here. No amount of believing that he lived the life he lived will take any one into the heavenly state, but *living the life that Jesus lived* will take every one who lives it there, in any age and in any clime, even whether or not he knows that such a man as Jesus ever lived.

The world has less need for a perverted and hence perverting doctrine of "vicarious atonement" that bodies of men have formulated by either intentionally or ignorantly dragging the teachings, as also the life, of

the Master down to a purely material interpretation — less need, most truly, has the
world for this perverting doctrine than it
has for the great vitalising fact of a conscious, living at-one-ment with the Father's
life, as every one whose spiritual sense is
at all unfolded will inevitably get from the
life and teachings of the Master, if indeed
he is more interested in the real living truth
that he taught than he is in the almost
numberless man-made theological theories
and dogmas regarding it.

In order that we may ever keep our standing ground clearly in mind, let us now gather
into a single view the substance of what we
have endeavoured thus far to present.

From everlasting to everlasting is Being,
self-existent, without beginning and without
end.   Depending upon nothing outside of
itself and the essential essence, the very life
of all that through it comes into existence,
it is therefore Infinite Being.   Existing at
first as pure spirit, it is therefore Divine
Being.   Literally the I Am, the Divine
Jehovah, the Infinite God.   Then, animated
by love and acting through its own volition,

it projects itself into existence and assumes the various forms we see in the universe about us, including ourselves. But by the act of projecting itself into existence, the Infinite Divine Being does not change in the least its essential inner nature, as indeed it would be impossible for it to do. What, then, in reality is there in existence? Only Divine Being, the Infinite God in all his manifold manifestations; and thus it remains through all eternity, as must necessarily be from its very nature, and otherwise it could not be. God, then, is the Infinite Being, the Infinite Spirit which is the essential essence, the life of all, which therefore fills all the universe with Himself alone, so that all is He, since He is all.

But when Divine Being incarnates itself in flesh and forms for its use a physical body — a human body, as we call it — it necessarily has to manifest through the instrumentality of physical senses, and, though Divine Being is infinite, the vision of man is limited, and for a time his true inner Life (always Divine Being) is concealed from him, for he naturally interprets everything from the standpoint of the physical. First that

which is natural, and man knows himself
only as a natural physical being, differing
not essentially from the material universe
about him.   As he looks out, however, he
sees that he differs from other forms in existence, in that he has a mind through which
thought is engendered, a mind that grows by
using.   Then contemplating himself and
longing for the truth of his existence,
gradually there dawns upon his consciousness the fact that his life is Divine Being,
that other than this it has never been—except
in his own mind when in his thought he
mistook the mere physical form in existence
as the real essential life itself, thus separating
his life from the Infinite Divine Life.   He
thus realises that in God he lives, moves,
and has his being, that God is the life
of his life, his very life itself; and thus
he comes in time into the conscious,
living realisation of his oneness with the
Infinite Life and Power.   And so we find
it true—first the natural man, then the
spiritual.

Through thought, and through thought
alone, the second man, the Lord from
Heaven, is gradually evolved out of the

first man, which is of the earth earthy.
Through a perfectly natural process of
evolution, out of the first man Adam —
sense perception — is evolved the Christ
man — Divine self-realisation.   Impossible,
however, is it for anything to be evolved
that was not first involved; and so man
finds that the Lord Christ has always been
within and he has known it not.

It is the same to-day as it was many years
ago with Jacob when he said, "Surely the
Lord is in this place; and I knew it not."
This and all that followed he found simply
by using the stones of the place where he
was; for with the stones of the place he
made for himself a pillow, and it was while
sleeping on this pillow that he beheld the
ladder set upon the earth and reaching to
the heavens, upon which the angels were
ascending and descending, and thus it was
that he entered into communion with the
life of the heavens.   Later, then, he transformed the pillow into a pillar that served
as a guide to other men.

And so with every human soul—we must
use simply the stones of the place where we
are.   The only stones with which human

life can build is thought.   It and it alone
is the moulding, the creative power —
earnest, sincere thought of the place where
we are, this constitutes the stones of the
place where we are and with which we
can make a pillow upon which for the
time being to rest.   Through this and this
alone will the life of the heavens be
opened to us; for angels ascending —
aspiration — will in time bring to us angels
descending—inspiration.   Then with Jacob
of old we will cry out, " Behold, the Lord
is in this place; and I knew it not."
Then our pillow, the thought that gives
us the knowledge that the Infinite Divine
Life is always within, the Essential Essence
of the human soul itself, we can convert
into a pillar, a pillar that will be a guide
to lead other men into the same realisation
and life.

And so the entire problem of human life
is wonderfully simple and easy if we are
but true to the highest within us, and keep
ourselves free from the various perplexing
and mystifying theological theories and
dogmas, which ordinarily give merely a
promise of spiritual awakening, realisation,

and power in some other form of life, rather than actualising it here and now in this life.

But only as man becomes conscious of the Lord Christ within, only as he becomes conscious,—realises in thought that he is one with the Infinite Life and Power,— does this great fact become a moving and mighty force in the affairs of his daily life. Until this is true he remains in the condition of the eagle, which, though unchained, thinking nevertheless that he was still chained, remained in captivity when the freedom of the heavens awaited simply the spreading of his wings.

Although the answer to our title has been given both in lines and between lines long before this, it may be an aid to us, especially in making practical what is to follow, to put it as best we can into a definite form: The greatest thing ever known—indeed, the greatest thing that ever can be known—is that in our real essential nature we are one with the Infinite Life and Power, and that by coming into, and dwelling continually in, the *conscious, living realisation* of this great fact, we enable to be manifested unto us and actualised within us the qualities and powers of the Divine Life, and this in the exact degree of the completeness of this realisation on our part.

II

DIVINE ENERGIES IN EVERY-DAY LIF.

AND what, let us ask, is the result and hence the value of this realisation? For unless it is of value in the affairs of every-day life, it is then a mere dead theory, and consequently of no real value. *Use* must be the final test of everything, and if it has no actual use, or if no visible results follow its use, we had better not spend time with it, for it is then not founded upon truth.

First, let it be said, it is not the mere intellectual recognition, merely the dead theory, but the conscious, vital and living realisation of this great truth, that makes it of value, and that makes it show forth in the affairs of every-day life. This it is, and this alone, that gives true blessedness, for this is none other than the finding of the kingdom of God, and when this is once found and lived in, all other things literally and necessarily follow. Through this the qualities and powers of the Divine Life are more and more realised and actualised, and through their leading we are led into the possession of all other things.

He who comes into this full and living realisation of his oneness with the Divine Life is brought at once into right relations with himself, with his fellow-men, and with the laws of the universe about him. He lives now in the inner, the real life, and whatever is in the interior must necessarily take form in the exterior, for all life is from within out. There is no true life in regard to which this law does not hold. And if the will of God is done in the inward life, then is it necessarily done in all things of the outward life, and the results are always manifest. Thus and thus alone it is that men have become prophets, seers, and saviours; they have become what the world calls the "elect" of God, because in their own lives they first elected God and lived their lives in His life. And thus it is that to-day men can become prophets, seers, and saviours, for the laws of the Divine Life and the relations of what we term the human life to it are identically the same to-day as they have been in all time past and will be in all time to come. The Divine Being changes not; it is man alone who changes.

It is solely by virtue of man's leaving the inner life of the spirit and thus departing from God, or by virtue of his not yet finding this real life, that sin and error, pain and disease, fears and forebodings, have crept as naturally and as necessarily as that effect follows cause into his life; only by closing his eyes to the inner light, by shutting his ears to the inner voice, that, although he has eyes to see, yet he sees not, and, although he has ears to hear, yet he hears not. And it is only by uniting his life with the Divine Life, and thus living again the life of the spirit, that these things will go, even as they have come.

All the evil, unhappiness, misery, and want in the world are attributable to man, and are the direct results of his taking his life, either consciously or unconsciously, either directly or indirectly, out of harmony with the Power that works for righteousness and consequently for wholeness and perfection. And when our life is lived in the life of God, and God's will therefore becomes our will, all is and necessarily must be well with us, for contrary to His will it is impossible that anything should ever come to pass. And thus it is that he who seeks first the kingdom of God and His righteousness shall have all other things added unto him. The soul, the real life, is Divine, and by allowing it to become translucent to Infinite Spirit by living continually in this conscious union with Divine Being it reveals all things to us. Things become hidden, mysteries fill and uncertainties pervade life only as we turn away from the inner light and life; there is nothing that is hidden of itself; to God all things are known, and he who consciously lives his life in the life of God sees with the Divine vision that reveals all things to him. He who lives continually under this Divine guidance enters thereby into the realm of the highest wisdom, and even in the most trivial things of every-day life he never finds himself in a state of doubt or perplexity, for he always knows what to do and how to do it.

He has no regrets for the past, because

before he entered into his present consciousness he was in a sense dead unto life, and
all regrets that he might have for the past
'are now swallowed up in the joys that the
new birth that has brought him into fulness
of life continually spreads before his every
step. He has neither fears nor forebodings
in regard to the future, for he knows that
contrary to God's will, which is now his
will, nothing can ever come to pass. Peace,
therefore, a full and abiding peace, is continually his.

As all life is from within out, and as this
is absolutely true in regard to the physical
body, the fountain of Divine Life that has
been opened up within him, which of itself
can admit of no disease or imperfection of
any kind, will allow only healthy conditions
to be externalised in his body; and where
unhealthy conditions have been built into it
before his entrance into the new life, the life
that now courses through it will in time
drive them out by entirely replacing the
diseased structure with that which is pure
and whole.

A continually growing sense of power is
his, for he is now working in conjunction

C

with the Infinite God, and with God all things are possible. In material things he is not lacking, for all things are from this one Infinite Source, and, guided by the Divine Wisdom and sustained by the Divine Power that are now his, in a perfectly natural and normal way he finds that an abundance of all things is his, always in hand in sufficient time to supply all his material needs, and never is there lack when the time comes, if he simply does each day what his hands find to do. Sure always of this unfailing source of supply, he does not give himself to the accumulation and the hoarding of great material possessions, thereby robbing and enslaving the real life.

His thoughts grow more and more into the nature of their Divine Source, and as *thoughts are forces*, and as in the degree that they are spiritualised do they become ever more effective in their operations, so through their instrumentality is he able to mould more and more effectively the every-day conditions of life. And so as he enters into this new life he finds that all things of the outer life fall into line; for *as is the inner, so always and necessarily is the outer.*

These truths will come as new revelations to many, and again to many they will come merely as agents to strengthen and possibly to arouse to renewed life the realisations of which they are already more or less conscious. In themselves, however, they are not new, *but as old as the world.* They are the real spirit of true Christianity, not, however, of the Christianity that the majority of people conventionally hold, which in many respects is as radically inconsistent as it is void of results, but the great transcendent truths of our relations with the Father's life that Jesus taught.

They are likewise the real essential spirit of all the great religions of the world, and as all religions in their purity are from the same source,—God speaking through the minds of those who have come into a sufficient union with Him to hear and to interpret His voice, the one universal source of all true inspiration and all true revelation,—so far as their fundamental principles are concerned they are necessarily the same.

And the great spiritual awakening, the beginnings of which we are witnessing in all parts of the world to-day, is evidence that the Divine Breath is stirring in the minds and hearts of men and women in a manner such as it has rarely if ever stirred before. Men and women are literally finding God. They are breaking through the mere letter and form of an old and too-long-held ecclesiastical theorising and dogmatism into the real vital spirit of the religion of the living and transcendent God. They are waking here and there and everywhere to the realisation of their oneness with the living God. Their lives are being completely filled with this realisation, and as a consequence they are showing forth the works of God.

They are leaving the old one-day-in-seven, some-other-world religion, and they are finding the joys as well as the practicability of an every-day, this-world religion. They are passing out of the religion of death and possible glory hereafter, into the religion of life and joy and glory here and now, to-day and every day, as well as hereafter and forevermore. With this new religion of the living God and the spiritual power that through it is being made active in their lives, they are moulding in detail all of the affairs of every-day life, proving thereby that their religion is the religion of life. And any system of religion that does not enable its possessor to do this is simply *not* religion, and we should no longer desecrate the word by applying it to any such hollow mockeries.

To this old semblance of religion those who are thus entering into this new and larger religion of life will never return, nor can they, any more than the chick can enter within the confines of its shell again after it has been once born into life. Having found the pearl, the shell for them must perish ; or rather, as it is of no farther value to them, it perishes simply by the operation of natural law. Centred thus in the Infinite, working now in conscious harmony with Divine forces, they ever after rule the world from within.

III

THE MASTER'S GREAT BUT LOST GIFT

THE conclusions we have arrived at thus far we have arrived at independently of any authority outside of our own reason and insight. It is always of interest as well as of greater or less value to compare our own conclusions with those of others whose opinions we value. It would indeed be a matter of exceeding great interest to compare those we have reached with those of a number whose opinions come with greater or less authority to all the world. Space does not permit this, however, and I propose that we give the balance of our time to the consideration, though necessarily brief consideration, of two such; one universally regarded as one of the most highly illumined teachers, if not the most highly illumined, the world has ever known, the Christ Jesus; the other universally regarded as one of the most highly illumined philosophers the world has ever known, the philosopher Fichte.

And in these two we have the advantage of the life and teachings of one who lived and taught nearly nineteen hundred years ago, and one who lived and taught a trifle less than a hundred years ago. By selecting these, let it also be said, we have the advantage of two whose lives fully manifested the truth of that which they taught.

In considering the life and teachings of Jesus, let us consider them not as dull expositors interpret and represent them, but as he himself gave them to the world. Certainly Jesus was Divine; but he was Divine, as he himself clearly taught, in just the same sense that you and I and every human soul is Divine. He differed from us, however, in that he had come into a far clearer and fuller realisation of his divinity than we have come into, as indeed his life so clearly indicates. Jesus *was* God manifest in the flesh, as indeed every one must be who comes into the full realisation of his oneness with God, as Jesus himself again so clearly taught.

In the thoroughly absurd, illogical, and positively demoralising doctrine of "vicarious atonement," as given us by early ecclesiastical bodies by perverting the real teachings of Jesus even to the extent of calling interpolations in the New Testament to their aid, we certainly cannot believe. Many do, however, believe that it has done more harm to the real teachings of Jesus, has been more productive of scepticism and infidelity, than all other causes combined. It is a doctrine that can be formulated only by those who have no spiritual insight themselves, and who therefore drag the teachings of the Master down to a purely material interpretation because of their inability to give them the spiritual interpretation that he intended they should have.

If his mission was not that of vicarious atonement, not for the purpose of appeasing the wrath and indignation of an angry God and thus reconciling Him to His children, what then was it? Clearly his mission was that of a Redeemer as he gave himself out to be—a Redeemer to bring the children of men back to their Father. And how did he purpose to do this? Clearly by having them consciously unite their lives with the Father's life, even as he had united his. The kingdom of God and His righteousness is not only what he came to teach, but what he clearly and unmistakably taught.

That he plainly and unequivocally taught his disciples that this was his mission is evidenced by numerous sentences such as the following, occurring all through the gospels: Matt. iv. 23, "Jesus went about in all Galilee, teaching in their synagogues and preaching the gospel of the kingdom," etc. . . . Luke viii. 1, "He went about through cities and villages, preaching and bringing the good tidings of the kingdom of God." . . . Luke iv. 43, "But he said unto them: I must preach the good tidings of the kingdom of God to other cities also, *for therefore was I sent*." . . . Luke ix. 2, "And he sent them forth to preach the kingdom of God and to heal the sick." . . . Matt. xxiv. 14, "And this gospel of the kingdom shall be preached in the whole world, for a testimony unto all nations," etc. . . . In more than thirty places in the first three gospels do we find Jesus thoroughly explaining to his disciples his especial mission—to preach the glad tidings of the coming of the kingdom of God; and even before he entered upon his public work, we hear John the Baptist going before him and saying, "Repent ye; for the kingdom of Heaven is at hand."

What did Jesus mean by the kingdom of God, or, as he sometimes expressed it, the kingdom of Heaven? As an answer, and an answer better than any speculations in regard to it, let us again take his own words: "Neither shall they say, Lo here! or, Lo there! for, behold, the kingdom of God is within you." He taught only what he himself had found, the conscious union with the Father's life as the one and all-inclusive thing. With Jesus from the very first, only in union with God was there reality. And this life in the Father's life seemed nothing at all marvellous to him; it was perfectly natural, and the only life he knew. Hence he could not say otherwise than that he and the Father were one. His vision was so clear and his already realised Divine life was so full and complete, that he knew that it was utterly impossible for his life to be without the Father's life, as *we* indeed shall know when our vision becomes clear and we enter into the same fully realised union with it.

This great knowledge came to Jesus not through intellectual speculation and still less through any communication from without; it came to him through his own interior consciousness; to all appearances he was born with it. He was born with a peculiar aptitude for discerning things of the Spirit, just as among us some are born with a peculiar aptitude for one thing and others for other things. But so great was this power naturally in Jesus that in it we may justly say he had a great advantage over most people born into the world, and for this reason was he all the more able and all the greater reason was there for him to be one of the great world Teachers and hence Redeemers. He was indeed Immanuel—God with us.

Jesus, I repeat, never speaks of his life in any other connection than as one with the Father's life.

In reply to a question from Thomas in the fourteenth chapter of John, he says, " If ye had known me, ye would have known my Father also: from henceforth ye know him and have seen him." Philip, who was standing near, unable to comprehend the interior meaning of the Master's words, said unto him : " Lord, show us the Father, and it sufficeth us." Jesus, somewhat surprised that he had not made himself clear to them, replied : " Have I been so long time with you, and dost thou not know me, Philip? He that hath seen me hath seen the Father ; how sayest thou, Show us the Father? Believest thou not that I am in the Father, and the Father in me? The words I speak unto you I speak not from myself : but the Father abiding in me doeth His work. Believe me that I am in the Father and the Father in me : or believe me for the very works' sake."

But if his especial mission was to preach the good tidings of the kingdom of God, why, I hear it asked, did he claim that only through *him* can we come unto the kingdom, as he indeed says in his conversation with Philip and Thomas immediately preceding the part just quoted : " I am the way, the truth, and the life ; no one cometh unto the Father but by me." Simply because it was the living truth that he brought, which was and evermore is to redeem men by uniting them in mind and heart with the Father. His realised oneness with the Father's life was the way, the truth, and the life, and only by going over the same path that he himself had trod can anyone be truly united with the Father. He found this great, vital and redeeming truth nowhere else in the world; he had to speak as one standing alone, and in this sense he spoke most truly and most literally when he said, " No one cometh unto the Father but by me." And in order to point out his life, his realised oneness with the Father's life, as the way, the truth, and the life, he spoke and indeed had to speak as he did, even at the risk of being misunderstood and having his words taken in a purely material sense, as was the tendency of the spiritual poverty of the age, and indeed as his very disciples so often interpreted his words, as we have but recently seen. In order to give forth the spiritual teachings which he gave, he had to use the language and the illustrations that their material minds could grasp, and in this way make his teachings doubly liable to a purely material interpretation.

"I am the bread of life," said he to those assembled about him ; " your fathers did eat the manna in the wilderness, and they died.

This is the bread which cometh down out of heaven, that a man may eat thereof, and not die. I am the *living* bread which came down out of heaven: if any man eat of this bread, he shall live forever: yea, and the bread which I will give is my flesh, for the life of the world." The Jews taking his words in a material sense argued one with another and said: "How can this man give us his flesh to eat?" Jesus simply reaffirmed his statement, saying: "Verily, verily, I say unto you, except ye eat the flesh of the Son of man and drink his blood, ye have not life in yourselves. . . . For my flesh is meat indeed, and my blood is drink indeed." Literally, "My flesh is the true food, and my blood is the true drink. He that eateth my flesh and drinketh my blood abideth in me and I in him. As the living Father sent me, and I live because of the Father, so he that eateth me, he also shall live because of me."

And many of his disciples, even, when they heard him speaking in this way, said among themselves, "This is a hard saying; who can hear him?"—who can understand him? Jesus, quickly perceiving that they were again dragging his words down to a material

interpretation, asked them if what he had
just said caused them to stumble, *and then,
in order that they get his real meaning,* he
said, "It is the spirit that quickeneth ; the
flesh profiteth nothing: the *words* that I
have spoken unto you are spirit and are life."
And so all except those who are wholly
spiritually, not to say even mentally, blind,
can readily see that what Jesus meant to say,
and what he actually did say, was, the words
that he spoke to them of his oneness with the
Father's life were the true meat and the true
drink, of which, unless a man ate and drank,
he had not life in himself, but that these
were able to give him life and life eternal.

"He that eateth my flesh and drinketh my
blood abideth in me, and I in him." Or,
reversing the expression, He that dwelleth
in me and I in him, he it is that eateth
my flesh and drinketh my blood. "The
words that I have spoken unto you, (they)
are spirit and (they) are life." "As the
living Father hath sent me, and I live because of the Father, so he that eateth me,
he also shall live because of me." In the
words of another,[1] "To eat his flesh and

[1] Fichte in "The Way towards the Blessed Life."

drink his blood means to become wholly and entirely he himself; to become altogether changed into his person without reserve or limitation ; to be a faithful repetition of him in another personality; to be transubstantiated with him, *i.e.*, as he is the Eternal Word made flesh and blood, to become his flesh and blood, and what follows from that, and indeed is the same thing, to become the very Eternal Word made flesh and blood itself; to think wholly and entirely like him, and so as if he himself thought and not we ; to live wholly and entirely like him, and so as if he himself lived in our life. As surely as you do not now attempt to drag down my own words, and reduce them to the narrow meaning that Jesus is only to be imitated, as an unattainable pattern, partially and at a distance, as far as human weakness will allow, but accept them in the sense in which I have spoken them, that we must be transformed into Christ himself, so surely will it become evident to you that Jesus could not well have expressed himself otherwise, and that he actually did express himself excellently well. Jesus was very far from representing himself as that unattainable ideal into which he was first transformed by the spiritual poverty of the after-ages; nor did his apostles so regard him."

To live in Christ is to live the life he lived, by living in the truth in which he lived and which he taught. The one great truth in which he continually lived was, as we have seen, that only in conscious union with God is there any real life, and therefore we can readily see why he continually gave out, as the Gospel writers tell us so many times he did, that his especial mission was to preach the glad tidings of the kingdom of God. Were it not possible for us to live the same life that he lived, he certainly would not have taught what he taught. This wonderful life of fully realised Divine life Jesus claims not for himself alone, but for all who actually live in the truth that he taught.

It was not to establish any material institution, as the church, that Jesus made his mission, but that the kingdom of God and His righteousness should become actualised and hold sway in the minds and hearts of men — this was his mission, an entirely

D

different thing from the founding of a material organisation. Paul and his party, sharing the then prevailing ideas that a material kingdom was to be established, were the originators of the church, not Jesus. We find the word "church" mentioned in the four Gospels by Jesus only once or twice, and then only in an incidental way, while we find the kingdom mentioned over thirty times in the first three Gospels alone.

As we have already pointed out, had it been his purpose to establish a material organisation, then he certainly would not have given it out that something else was his especial purpose. But when the material organisation, the church, purely a man-made institution, was established, the early church fathers bringing even interpolations of the Holy Word to their aid in establishing it and some of its various observations,—as modern scholarship has already so clearly discovered, and as it is continually discovering,—the following ages, thinking that they had an institution to keep up, gradually lost, to a greater or less extent, the real spiritual teachings of the Master in their zeal to keep

up the form of an institution with which he
had nothing to do. And those long and
bitter persecutions of the church in the
early and middle ages, as well as the long
list of crimes sanctioned and committed
directly by the church of the middle ages,
show that they had not the real truth; for
those who live in the truth and have it
uppermost in their minds and hearts never
persecute — only those who are on either
uncertain or false ground, and whose en-
deavour it is to keep up the form of an
institution which they feel would otherwise
fall to the ground.

No, true religion has never been known
either to persecute or to show intolerance
of any kind. Throughout the whole history
of the churches' heresies and persecutions,
the persecuted party has ever occupied a
correspondingly higher and the persecuting
party a lower position, the persecuting party
continually fighting as it were for life. But
the *real truth* that Jesus taught will not
cause nor will it even permit persecutions—
hence we find the latter only where there
is the lack of the former.

And again, the *real truth* that Jesus taught

will not admit of divisions, much less of intolerance, for all real truth is exact truth, and in regard to it there can be no differences, and our modern theologians, and our churches of to-day, which get their form and life from the speculations and theories of the former, certainly have not the real truth that Jesus taught, for they are divided in various directions on practically every dogma that they seek to promulgate. And strange as it may seem, heresy trials, with all their absurd attendant features, are not entirely unknown even yet to-day. But in Jesus' own words, " A house divided against itself cannot stand." And so if the church of to-day wants to stand as a real power in the world, or if indeed it wants to stand at all, it must either get back to, or it must come up, as the case may be, to the *real living truth* that Jesus lived and taught. Unless it does this it will inevitably lose its hold on the people even more rapidly than it is losing it to-day. And certainly the younger ones whom it does not yet hold will not be drawn to it, when they can turn to that which has a thousand-fold more of truth and hence of life-giving power than it has to offer.

That this is not a mere sentiment on our part is evidenced by the wonderful rapidity with which the "New Thought" movement —would that we could designate what we mean without using any term—which has, as its underlying truth, this conscious union with the Divine Life and the actualised powers attendant upon it as Jesus taught,— hence not a new discovery, but a recovery, —is growing in America, in England, to be brief, in practically every civilised country in the world. Thousands every year in our own and in other countries are finding in it the joys of the realised Divine Life, and are turning to it from that which but poorly feeds them ; and that this also is no mere sentiment on our part is evidenced by the contents of a letter recently sent by a noted divine in high official standing in the church in England to a noted American preacher, in which he said, in substance, that the church in England is literally honeycombed by the "New Thought" movement, and asked that he might have sent a list of the best books that had already appeared in America along the lines indicated.

And so what we need to-day is the same

as what the world is eagerly calling for, the life-giving power of the great central truth that the Master taught, and not the various theories and speculations in regard to his origin, his birth, his life, and the meaning of his teachings. And still less, the fabrications of the early fathers in regard to inherited sin, original sin, vicarious atonement, and their believe-and-be-saved doctrine, and the alternative doctrine, fail to believe that which is opposed to all reason, all common-sense, all real mercy, as well as all true justice, and be damned, be forever and eternally lost.

Jesus is indeed a lamb of God that taketh away the sins of the world, but he takes them away by bringing to the world the truth that shall make men free. Hence it is through his life and the truth that he lived and taught, not through his death and the observance of the various ceremonies and forms that have grown up around it. Those who are aided by symbols—and I am aware of the fact that for some, many hallowed associations are connected with them—may do well to make use of them until they outgrow the need for them. But symbols

are of value only where the real thing is not,
and those who have the real thing no longer
have need for symbols. "But the hour
cometh," said Jesus, "and now is" (since I
have brought you the real spirit of truth),
"when the true worshippers shall worship
the Father in spirit and truth ; for such doth
the Father seek to be His worshippers.
God is a Spirit, and they that worship Him
must worship in spirit and truth."

Jesus, according to his own words, did
not propose to rest satisfied with the mere
historical belief that he was the Eternal Word
made flesh, and much less, as some phases
of theology teach, that reconciliation with
the Father, as ordinarily understood, was his
purpose. God would adopt no methods in
connection with His children that are opposed to their own reason. Nor would He
adopt any partial, limited, or tribal methods.

And if, as various theologians would have
us believe, that reconciliation with the Father
can come about only by a belief in the shed-
ding of the material, physical blood of Jesus,
that through it the Father may receive satis-
faction for His favour, how is it in regard
to the great company of those who cannot

accept a theory so absurd, so illogical, and
so opposed to the nature of the living God
whom they *know*, and about whom they
no longer have to speculate and theorise,
to say nothing of the millions upon millions
of those who never have heard, and other
millions who never can hear, of the man
Jesus and the story of his blood "shed for
the sins of the world," nine-tenths of whom,
for good reasons, would not believe it if they
did hear it? No, these fabrications cannot
be true, for "in every nation, he that feareth
God and worketh righteousness is accepted
of Him." And so one may be without connection with any church, and even without
connection with any *established* religion, and
yet be in spirit, hence in reality, a much
truer Christian than hosts of those who
profess to be his most ardent followers, as
indeed Jesus himself so many times says.
"By their *fruits* ye shall know them," said
he. "Not every one that saith unto me,
Lord, Lord, shall enter into the kingdom
of heaven; but he that *doeth* the will of my
Father which is in heaven."

That which calls itself Christianity must
prove itself, and only that which shows forth

in its life the works, the power, the influence
—the truth that Jesus' life showed forth—is
the real. "He that believeth on me," said
Jesus,—and shows it by *living* my life,—
"the works that I do shall he do also; and
greater works than these shall he do because
I go unto the Father." And he who would
know by what authority Jesus spoke, let him
live the life that he lived and he will then
know of the doctrine. Thus and thus only
can it be known. We may speculate and
theorise in regard to it, but only by living
the life can we *know it*.

IV

THE PHILOSOPHER'S RIPEST LIFE THOUGHT

LET us now see how the truths we have already set forth stand in reference to the thought of the philosopher Fichte. Truth, the highest truth, and truth for its own sake, was the one supreme object of his life. And in order to discern this clearly himself, that he in turn might point it out clearly to others, he stood erect and alone, free from connection with any institution, organisation, or system of thought that would distort or limit his vision and induce him either intentionally or unintentionally to interpret truth by bending it to suit the tenets of the system of thought or the institution to which he might be, even though inadvertently, bound.

It was of Fichte that an eminent English scholar once said: "Far above the dark vortex of theological strife in which punier intellects chafe and vex themselves in vain, Fichte struggles forward in the sunshine of pure thought which sectarianism cannot see, because its weakened vision is already filled with a borrowed and imperfect light." ⌣

It is, moreover, always of value to know how the truth that one finds and endeavours to give to others finds embodiment in his own life, for this is the sure and unfailing test of its vitality, if not indeed of its reality. A word or two, therefore, in reference to the life of Fichte may not be inappropriate here, a word or two from the same eminent English scholar quoted above, the translator of his works from the German to the English, for he knew well his life as he knew also his philosophy. "We prize his philosophy deeply," says he; "it is to us an invaluable possession, for it seems the noblest exposition to which we have yet listened of human nature and divine truth; but with reverent thankfulness we acknowledge a still higher debt, for he has left behind him the best gift which man can bequeath to man—a brave, heroic human life."

"In the strong reality of his life,—in his intense love for all things beautiful and true, —in his incorruptible integrity and heroic devotion to the right, we see a living mani-

festation of his principles. His life is the
true counterpart of his philosophy—it is that
of a strong, free, incorruptible man."

And now to a few paragraphs of Fichte's
thought bearing more or less directly upon
the theme immediately in hand. After setting forth in a very comprehensive manner
the truth in regard to Being, which he
identifies with Life much in the same
general manner as we have already endeavoured to set it forth, and then after
making it clear that by God he means this
Infinite Being, this Spirit of Infinite Life,
he says:

.   .   .   .

"God alone is, and nothing besides him,
—a principle which, it seems to me, may
be easily comprehended, and which is the
indispensable condition of all religious insight."

.   .   .   .

"But beyond this mere empty and
imaginary conception, and as we have
carefully set forth this matter above, God
enters into us in his actual, true, and
immediate life,—or, to express it more
strictly, we ourselves are this his immediate

Life. But we are not conscious of this
immediate Divine Life; and since, as we
have also already seen, our own Existence
—that which properly belongs to us—is that
only which we can embrace in consciousness,
so our Being in God, notwithstanding that
at bottom it is indeed ours, remains nevertheless forever foreign to us, and thus, in
deed and truth, *to ourselves* is not our Being;
we are in no respect the better of this insight,
and remain as far removed as ever from God.
We know nothing of this immediate Divine
Life, I said; for even at the first touch of
consciousness it is changed into a dead
World. . . . The form forever veils the
substance from us; our vision itself conceals
its object; our eye stands in its own light.
I say unto thee who thus complainest:
'Raise thyself to the standing-point of
Religion, and all these veils are drawn
aside; the World, with its dead principle,
disappears from before thee, and the Godhead once more resumes its place within
thee, in its first and original form, as Life,—
as thine own Life, which thou oughtest to
live and shalt live.'"

In setting forth how universally Divine

Being incarnates itself in human Life, he says: "From the first standing-point the Eternal Word becomes flesh, assumes a personal, sensible, and human existence, without obstruction or reserve, in all times, and in every individual man who has a living insight into his unity with God, and who actually and in truth gives up his personal life to the Divine Life within him,—precisely in the same way as it became incarnate in Jesus Christ."

Speaking, then, of the great fundamental fact that the truth that Jesus himself perceived and gave to the world, and also of the manner whereby he came into the perception of it, he says: "Jesus of Nazareth undoubtedly possessed the highest perception containing the foundation of all other Truth, of the absolute identity of Humanity with the Godhead, as regards what is essentially real in the former."

"His self-consciousness was at once the pure and absolute Truth of Reason itself, self-existent and independent, the simple fact of consciousness."

.   .   .   .

Then in showing that Jesus as he is pre-

sented to us by the apostle John never conceived of his life in any other light than
as one with the Father's Life, he says:

" But it is precisely the most prominent and
striking trait in the character of the Johannean
Jesus, ever recurring in the same shape, that
he will know nothing of such a separation
of his personality from his Father, and that
he earnestly rebukes others who attempt
to make such a distinction; while he con-
stantly assumes that he who sees him sees
the Father, that he who hears him hears the
Father, and that he and the Father are
wholly one; and he unconditionally denies
and rejects the notion of an independent
being in himself, such an unbecoming
elevation of himself having been made an
objection against him by misunderstanding.
To him Jesus was not God, for to him there
was no independent Jesus whatever; but
God was Jesus, and manifested himself as
Jesus."

To show, then, that this is a universal
truth, brought in its fulness, and with a living exemplified vitality, first to the world by
Jesus, but by no means applicable to him
alone, he says: " An insight into the absolute

unity of the Human Existence with the Divine is certainly the profoundest Knowledge that man can attain. Before Jesus this Knowledge had nowhere existed; and since his time, we may say, even down to the present day, it has been again as good as rooted out and lost, at least in profane literature."

That we must come into the same living realisation of this great transcendent truth that Jesus came into, either through his teaching and exemplified realisation of it, or through whatever channel it may come, he clearly indicates by the following: "The living possession of the theory we have now set forth—not the dry, dead, and merely historical knowledge of it—is, according to our doctrine, the highest, and indeed the only possible, Blessedness."

"The Metaphysical only, and not the Historical, can give us Blessedness; the latter can only give us understanding. If any man be truly united with God, and dwell in him, it is altogether an indifferent thing how he may have reached this state; and it would be a most useless and perverse employment, instead of living in the thing, to

be continually repeating over our recollec-
tions of the way. Could Jesus return into
the world, we might expect him to be
thoroughly satisfied, if he found Christianity
actually reigning in the minds of men,
whether his merit in the work were recog-
nised or overlooked ; and this is, in fact, the
very least that might be expected from a
man who, while he lived on earth, sought
not his own glory, but the glory of him who
sent him."

And what in the eyes of Fichte are the
results that follow and hence the tests of
the genuineness of this higher realisation,
this True Religion, as he sometimes terms
it ? His words in this connection are : " True
Religion, notwithstanding that it raises the
view of those who are inspired by it to its own
region, nevertheless retains their Life firmly
in the domain of action, and of right moral
action. The true and real Religious Life is
not alone percipient and contemplative, does
not merely brood over devout thoughts, but
is essentially active. It consists, as we have
seen, in the intimate consciousness that God
actually lives, moves, and perfects his work
in us. If therefore there is in us no real

E

Life, if no activity and no visible work pro-
ceed forth from us, then is God not active in
us.   Our consciousness of union with God
is then deceptive and vain, and the empty
shadow of a condition that is not ours;
perhaps the general, but lifeless, insight that
such a condition is possible, and in others
may be actual, but that we ourselves have,
nevertheless, not the least portion in it."

" Religion does not consist in mere devout
dreams, I said: Religion is not a business
by and for itself, which a man may practise
apart from his other occupations, perhaps
on certain fixed days and hours; but it is
the inmost spirit that penetrates, inspires,
and pervades all our Thought and Action,
which in other respects pursue their ap-
pointed course without change or interrup-
tion.   That the Divine Life and Energy
actually lives in us is inseparable from
Religion, I said."

To show, then, how completely at one in
his or her consciousness this truly religious
man or woman becomes, how his or her
own personal will is lost in, and so trans-
muted into, the Divine Will, as also the
calmness and tranquillity with which his or

her life forever thereafter flows along, he says: "The expression of the constant mind of the truly Moral and Religious man is this prayer: 'Lord! let but thy will be done, then is mine also done; for I have no other will than this—that thy will be done."

"This Divine Life now continually develops itself within him, without hindrance or obstruction, as it can and must develop itself only in him and his individuality; this alone it is that he properly wills; his will is therefore always accomplished, and it is absolutely impossible that anything contrary to it should ever come to pass."

"Whatever comes to pass around him, nothing appears to him strange or unaccountable—he knows assuredly, whether he understand it or not, that it is in God's World, and that there nothing can be that does not directly tend to Good. In him there is no fear for the Future, for the absolute fountain of all Blessedness eternally bears him on towards it; no sorrow for the Past, for in so far as he was not in God he was nothing, and this is now at an end, and since he has dwelt

in God he has been born into Light;
while in so far as he was in God, that
which he has done is assuredly right and
good. He has never aught to deny himself, nor aught to long for; for he is at
all times in eternal possession of the fulness of all that he is capable of enjoying.
For him all labour and effort have vanished;
his whole Outward Existence flows forth,
softly and gently, from his Inward Being,
and issues out into Reality without difficulty
or hindrance."

Speaking, then, of how we may at once
enter into and live in the full realisation
of this real life, and also of those who,
instead of entering immediately into the
Kingdom and thus finding the highest
happiness and joy here and now, are
expecting to find it in its completeness
after the transition we call death, he says:
"Full surely indeed there lies a Blessedness beyond the grave for those who have
already entered upon it here, and in no
other form or way than that by which they
can already enter upon it here in this
moment; but by mere burial man cannot
arrive at Blessedness—and in the future

life, and throughout the whole infinite range of all future life, they would seek for happiness as vainly as they have already sought it here, if they were to seek it in aught else than in that which already surrounds them so closely here below that throughout Eternity it can never be brought nearer to them—in the Infinite. And thus does the poor child of Eternity, cast forth from his native home, and surrounded on all sides by his heavenly inheritance which yet his trembling hand fears to grasp, wander with fugitive and uncertain step throughout the waste, everywhere labouring to establish for himself a dwelling place, but happily ever reminded, by the speedy downfall of each of his successive habitations, that he can find peace nowhere but in his Father's house."

Finally, speaking of how completely doubt and uncertainty are eliminated from the life of him who through the realisation of the truth we have set forth becomes thereby centred in the Infinite, he says: "The Religious man is forever secured from the possibility of doubt and uncertainty. In every moment he knows distinctly what he wills, and ought to will; for the innermost root of his life—his will—forever flows forth from the Divinity, immediately and without the possibility of error; its indication is infallible, and for that indication he has an infallible perception. In every moment he knows that in all Eternity he shall know what he shall will, and ought to will; that in all Eternity the fountain of Divine Love which has burst forth in him shall never be dried up, but shall uphold him securely and bear him on forever."

Such, then, in general, are fragments of the thought, and, let it be added, the ripest thought, of one who has exerted perhaps as great a direct influence upon the life of his own immediate as well as succeeding ages as any man who has ever lived. It is to Fichte that, to a very great extent, the German Empire owes the splendid educational system it has to-day. His thought began to exert its influence at the time when its educational system was falling into a state of chaos, and even the Empire itself by virtue of its recent losses was in a more or less uncertain condition. And, acting to a greater or less extent through the minds of Froebel and

Pestalozzi, his thought has aided in giving to the world the truest type of education it has yet seen, that that we know under the name kindergarten, which is slowly but surely working to revolutionise our present educational methods, which stand so sadly in need of a change even so radical.

If the truth and vitality of a man's thought are to be judged by its permanent as well as its immediate influence, surely the thought of Fichte found its life in the realms of the highest truth, through which alone real vitality comes, for it has exerted and is still exerting a most powerful life-giving influence, an influence, indeed, that will never end.

V

SUSTAINED IN PEACE AND SAFETY FOREVER

AT what now have we arrived, and what has been the process? From our own reason and insight, independently of all outside authority, we have found the great truth that a living insight into the fact of the essential unity of the human life with the Divine Life is the profoundest knowledge that man can attain to. This as a mere intellectual perception, however, as a mere dead theory, amounts to but little, if indeed, to anything at all, as far as bearing fruit in every-day life is concerned. It is the vital, living realisation of this great transcendent truth in the life of each one that makes it a mighty moving and moulding force in his life.

Then we have also found that this same great truth was the great central fact of both the life and the teachings of one who comes as authority to practically all the world, the Christ Jesus. That this was the one great truth in which he continually lived, that it was the secret of his unusual insight and power, and that it was also the great truth that he came to bring to the world, he distinctly tells us. That it was not only what he proclaimed that he came to teach, but also what he distinctly taught, we have likewise found.

We have found also that the ripest life thought of the philosopher Fichte—whose spiritual vision was so fully unfolded as to enable him to give to the world such a remarkable blending of the intellectual and the spiritual in his philosophy — was almost if not identically the same in reference to this great truth, as was also his thought in regard to the life and the power as well as the mission of Jesus.

And when I see day after day the wonderful results that follow in the lives of those who have entered into this living realisation, then I know that Jesus knew whereof he spoke when he gave the injunction, "Seek ye first the kingdom of God and his righteousness, and all these things shall be added unto you." Moreover, I do not believe, but

I know, that whoever through this realisation thus finds the kingdom of God will
find his words — that all else will follow
—literally and absolutely as well as necessarily true.   All will follow in a perfectly
natural and normal manner, in full accord-
ance with natural spiritual law.

He who goes thus directly to the mountain
top will find all things spread out before
him in the valley below.   He who thus
becomes centred in the Infinite will find
that to the same centre whence his inner
life issues, all things pertaining to his outer
material life will in turn be drawn.   The
beauty of holiness is one with the beauty
of wholeness.   To know but the One Life
is to live in the fact and the beauty of
wholeness; and where wholeness is, there
no lack of anything will be found.

If what we ordinarily term our Christian
churches, and if the preachers who stand
in their pulpits, would fully and universally
give themselves to the real message that
Jesus gave to the world, then we would
find that "the common people" would go
to them and hear them gladly; there would
then be no hard pressing social situation to

face, for the people would then have a living knowledge of the one great truth through which all other things would come.

This great transcendent truth, however, that was the very essence of the life and the teachings of Jesus, has been even in our churches as good as rooted out and lost. And shall we conclude that because it is practically lost the greater part of the time and attention of the preacher in the large majority of them is given to the empty, barren, inconsequential themes it is given to? Or is it because so much time and attention is given to the latter that there is no time left for the former? However this may be, it certainly is true that that to a greater or less extent to-day we find identically the same conditions that Jesus found, and that he continually tried so hard to do away with. "Full well," said he, "ye reject the commandment of God, that ye may keep your own tradition."

Many a student comes from our theological schools so steeped in theological speculations and in denominational dogmas that he hasn't the slightest conception of what the real mission of Jesus was. What wonder, then, that the church to which he goes soon becomes a dead shell from which the life has gone, into which those in love with life will no longer enter, a church whose chief concern very soon is, how to raise the minister's stipend? But once let these minor and inconsequential, not to say at times petty, foolish, and absurd, things be dropped, and let all time and attention be given to the great central truth that Jesus brought to the world, and we shall find that during the next one hundred years, ay, during the next fifty years, what will then be real Christianity will make more progress than what is now termed Christianity has made during all the nineteen hundred years it has been in the world. The fact that during all these hundreds of years it has not accomplished more than it has is quite good evidence that something essential is lacking in it.

The real soul-cry even of all Christendom to-day is the same as the injunction given by the native ministers of Japan to a noted representative of the Christian religion as he was leaving there not long ago: "Send us no more doctrines: we are tired of them. Send us Christ." And the only way that Christ can be sent is by sending the great central truth that he brought to the world, a truth so *world-wide*, so *universal*, that, so far even as the so-called various great religions are concerned, in regard to it there can be no differences, for from its very nature it is at the very foundation, indeed, the very life essence, of them all. And so it is true in this sense that there is essentially but one religion, the religion of the living God. For to live in the conscious realisation of the fact that God lives in us, is indeed the life of our life, and that in ourselves we have no independent life, and hence no power, is the one great fact of all true religion, even as it is the one great fact of human life. Religion, therefore, at its purest, and life at its truest, are essentially and necessarily one and the same.

It is only through this living realisation of the essential unity of our life with the Father's life that true blessedness, and even true peace and happiness, can be found. The sooner, then, that we come into it, and thus live the life of the spirit, the better, for neither will they come nor can they be found in any other way. There is, moreover, no time either in this form of life, or in any other form, when we can any more readily come into it, and thereby into all that follows, than we can at this very moment.   And when this fountain of Divine Life is once fully opened within us, it can never again be dried up, and we can rest assured that it will at all times uphold us in peace and bear us on in safety.   And however strange or unaccountable at times occurrences may appear, we can rest in a triumphant security, knowing that only good can come, for in God's life there is only good, and in God's life we are now living, and there we shall live forever.

A METHOD

THERE is a simple method which will aid us greatly in coming into the realisation we have been considering. So simple is it that thousands and indeed millions have passed it by, looking, as is so generally our custom, for agencies of at least apparently greater power; we so frequently and so universally forget that the greatest things in life are the most simple.

The method is this: wherever you are, whatever doing, walking along the street or through the fields, at work of any kind, falling off to or awaking from sleep, setting about any undertaking, in doubt as to what course to pursue at any particular time, in brief, whatever it may be, carry with you this thought: It is the Father that worketh in me, my Father works and I work. This is the thought so continually used by Jesus, who came into probably the fullest realisation of the oneness of his life with the God-life that any one who has lived in the world thus far has come into, and it is given because it is so simple.   From it each can make his own formula.   Jesus' term was "the Father."   Many will likewise find themselves naturally using the same term and will find it becoming very precious to them.   Others will find themselves using other terms for the same conception and thought: It is the Father that worketh in me, my Father works and I work.   In other words, It is the spirit of Infinite Life and Power that is behind all, working in and through all, the life and animating power of all,—God,—that worketh in me, and I do as I am directed and empowered by It.

In this way we open ourselves, and become consciously awake to the Infinite Life and Power that is ever waiting and ready to direct and work in our lives, if we will merely put ourselves into the attitude whereby It can work in them.   In this way we open ourselves so that It can speak and manifest to and through us.   This It is ever ready to do if we will but make for It the right conditions.   By carrying with us this thought, by holding ourselves in this attitude of mind consciously for a while, by repeating it even in so many words now and then at first, we will find it in time becoming our habitual thought, and will find ourselves living in it without the conscious effort that we have to make at first, and we will in time find ourselves almost unconsciously living in it continually. Thus God as a living pres- ence, as a guiding, animating power, becomes an actuality in our lives. The conscious presence of God in our lives, which is the essence, indeed the sum and substance of *all* religion, then becomes a reality, and all wisdom and all power will be given us as we are able to appropriate and use them wisely; if for merely selfish, personal ends, they will be withheld; if for the greatest aid and service for the world, we will find them continually increasing.

With this higher realisation comes more and more the simple, child-like spirit. With Jesus we realise—Of myself I can do nothing, it is the Father within me that doeth His work. In ourselves we are and can do nothing; in God we can do all things. We never can be in the condition—in God— until through this higher realisation God becomes a *conscious, living* reality in our lives.

F

Faithfulness to this simple method will bring about a complete change in great numbers of lives. Each one for himself can test its efficacy in a very short time. It is the highway upon which many will enter and which will take them by easy stages into the realisation of the highest life that can be attained to. To set one's face in the right direction, and then simply to travel on, will in time bring him into the realisation of the highest life that can be even conceived of—it is the secret of all attainment.

For further suggestions as to the method of entering into this higher realisation, as also for a much fuller portrayal of its results in every-day life, the reader is directed to the volume by the same author entitled, "In Tune with the Infinite; or, Fullness of Peace, Power, and Plenty."

www.ingramcontent.com/pod-product-compliance
Lightning Source LLC
Chambersburg PA
CBHW020047030726
47499CB00007B/2624